DO YOU KNOW?™

Earth
and Nature

By
Cécile Benoist

Illustrated by
Robert Barborini
Adèle Combes
Beatrice Costamagna
Camille Tisserand

Twirl

Contents

Life on Our Planet 50

Taking Care of Earth 70

Index 92

 The "Let's Review!" pages at the end of each section help reinforce learning.

Index Quickly find the word you're looking for with the index at the end of the book.

Look for the colored boxes in the bottom right-hand corners. You will find references to related subjects in other parts of the book.

What Is Earth?

🌳 Life on Earth

Earth is our planet. We share it with millions of plants and animals on land and in water. The Sun provides Earth with light and warmth.

Sun

ocean

Earth

continent

How
do we stay put on Earth

The planet is round, but your feet stay firmly on the ground. This is also true for the people on the other side of the world.

When you jump, you don't stay up in the air. Your body comes back down because a force called gravity pulls you toward the ground.

Gravity also pulls the International Space Station toward Earth. The ISS moves in orbit faster than it "falls," so the astronauts look like they are floating.

The Solar System

Our solar system is made up of a star—the Sun—eight planets, and millions of smaller bodies, including dwarf planets, asteroids, and comets.

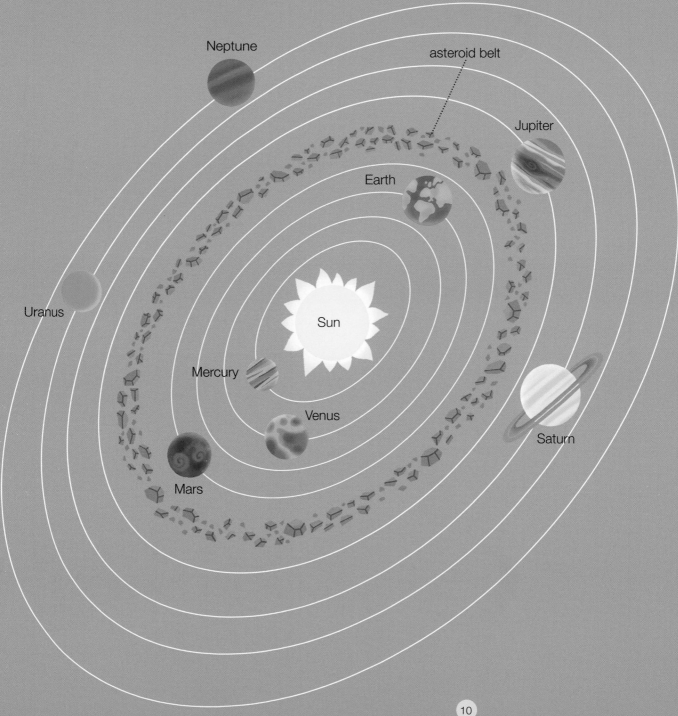

Neptune

asteroid belt

Jupiter

Earth

Uranus

Sun

Mercury

Venus

Saturn

Mars

Earth rotates on its own axis.

The axis is an imaginary line that goes from north to south through Earth's center.

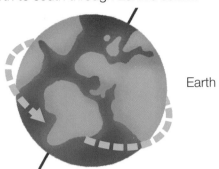

Earth

Earth revolves around the Sun.

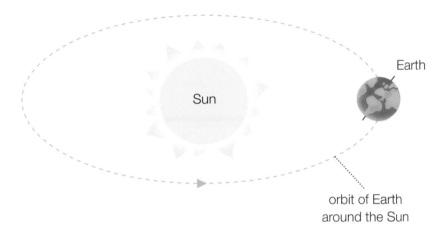

Sun

Earth

orbit of Earth around the Sun

The Moon revolves around Earth.

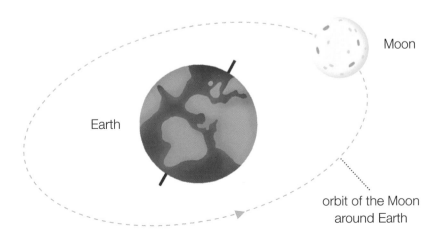

Moon

Earth

orbit of the Moon around Earth

Have you been on a playground spinner? Our planet spins in the same way, on its own axis. It takes a whole day for Earth to complete one turn.

The path that Earth takes around the Sun is called an orbit. It takes Earth an entire year to complete one revolution.

The Moon doesn't change its shape, but it looks different sometimes, depending on where it is in relation to Earth and the Sun.

Life on Earth **8** 🌱
Seasons **38** 🌱

● The Past

Since the birth of our planet about 4.6 billion years ago, many plants and animals have appeared and evolved.

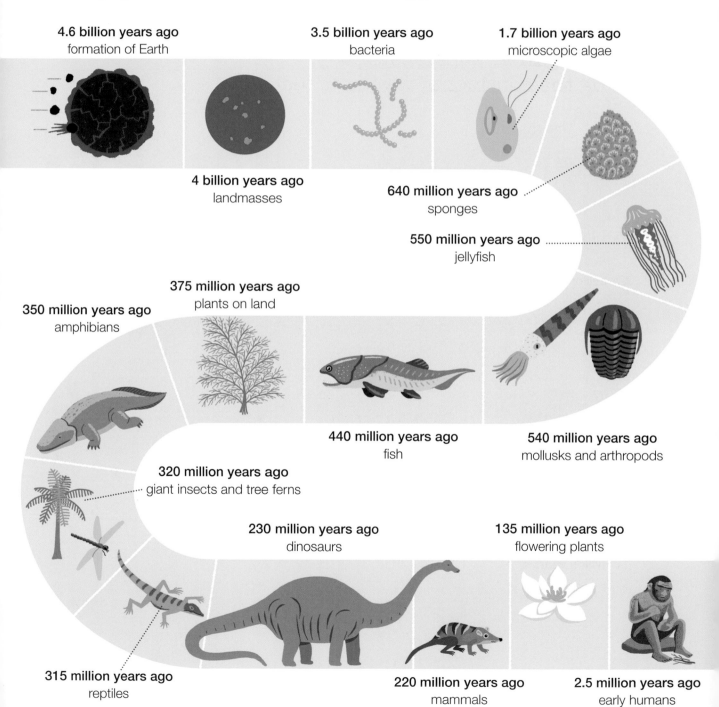

4.6 billion years ago
formation of Earth

3.5 billion years ago
bacteria

1.7 billion years ago
microscopic algae

4 billion years ago
landmasses

640 million years ago
sponges

550 million years ago
jellyfish

375 million years ago
plants on land

350 million years ago
amphibians

440 million years ago
fish

540 million years ago
mollusks and arthropods

320 million years ago
giant insects and tree ferns

230 million years ago
dinosaurs

135 million years ago
flowering plants

315 million years ago
reptiles

220 million years ago
mammals

2.5 million years ago
early humans

The Formation of Continents

A very long time ago, there was only one big expanse of land. Over time, the land began to separate slowly, becoming the continents we know today.

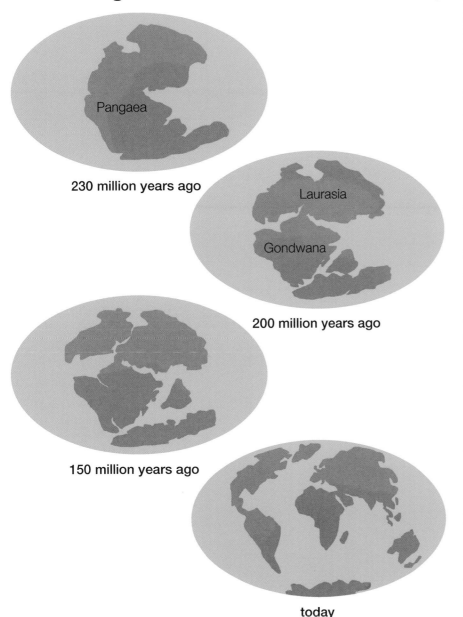

Pangaea

230 million years ago

Laurasia

Gondwana

200 million years ago

150 million years ago

today

In pictures of Earth from space, our planet looks like a ball that's mostly blue.

That is because oceans, seas, lakes, and other bodies of water cover almost three-quarters of the planet's surface, and water appears blue.

In small amounts, water looks clear. But when there's a lot, it is blue because of how water absorbs light and because it reflects the blue sky.

Continents

Continents are large areas of land. Asia is the biggest continent, both in size and in the number of people who live there.

North America

Atlantic Ocean

Europe

Africa

Pacific Ocean

South America

Southern Ocean

Arctic Ocean

Asia

Pacific Ocean

Indian Ocean

Australia

The Australian continent
is part of the region
of Oceania.

Antarctica

15

?

People live in a town or city that is in a state or province. The state or province is in a country, which is part of a continent.

Most continents are made up of a number of countries. There are more than 40 countries in the continent of Europe.

The continents of North and South America are connected by a narrow strip of land called an isthmus. Do you know which countries are in North America?

🧩 Tectonic Plates

The surface of Earth is made up of tectonic plates that fit together like puzzle pieces. Under these plates are different layers of rock, which surround the core.

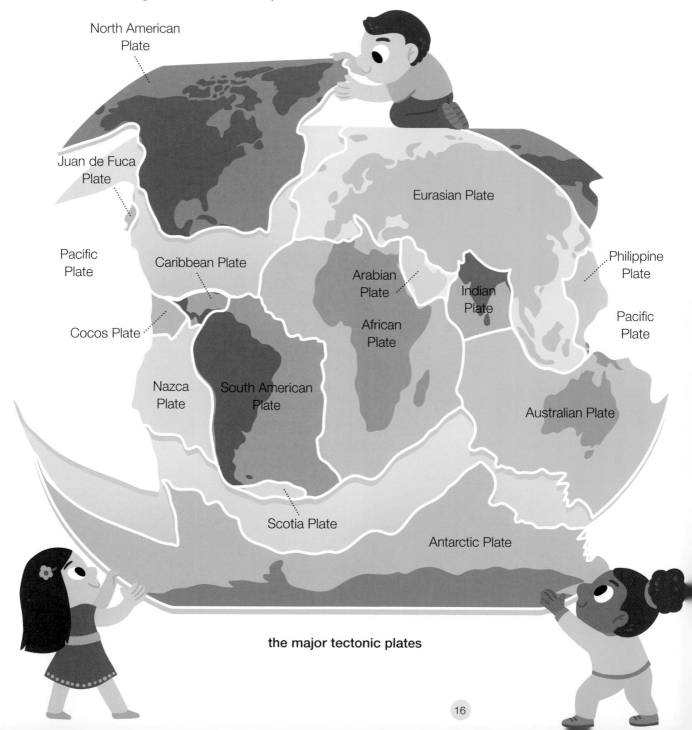

North American Plate

Juan de Fuca Plate

Pacific Plate

Caribbean Plate

Eurasian Plate

Arabian Plate

Indian Plate

Philippine Plate

Pacific Plate

Cocos Plate

African Plate

Nazca Plate

South American Plate

Australian Plate

Scotia Plate

Antarctic Plate

the major tectonic plates

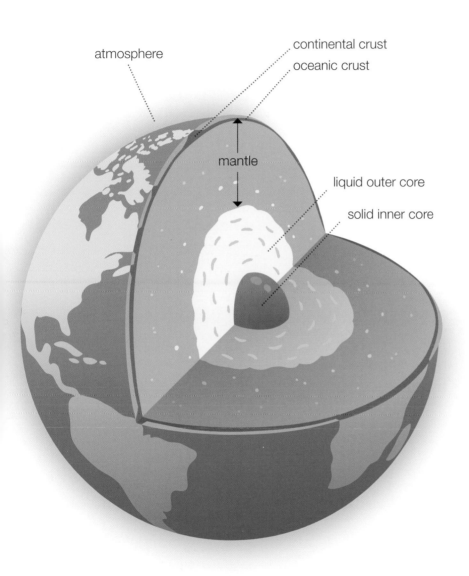

atmosphere

continental crust

oceanic crust

mantle

liquid outer core

solid inner core

Earth's layers

How
far is it to Earth's center ?

If you look inside a well, you may not be able to see the bottom. Maybe you'll wonder how far down it goes.

The center of our planet is almost 4,000 miles (6,500 kilometers) deep. It is also extremely hot, about 10,800°F (6,000°C).

Even if you can dig a deep hole, it's impossible to reach Earth's center or survive the heat.

⌃⌃ Movements of Earth

The tectonic plates are always moving, although very slowly. They can join together, pull apart, or even split. This means Earth's crust is always changing its shape.

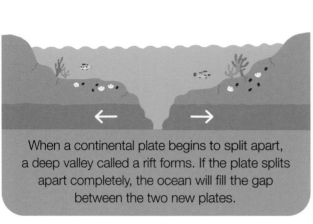

When a continental plate begins to split apart, a deep valley called a rift forms. If the plate splits apart completely, the ocean will fill the gap between the two new plates.

rift

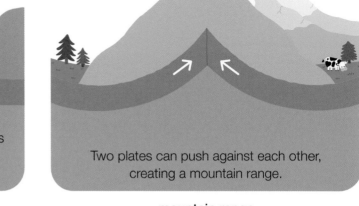

Two plates can push against each other, creating a mountain range.

mountain range

When two plates come together, one of them can sink down into the mantle.

A volcano forms.

volcano

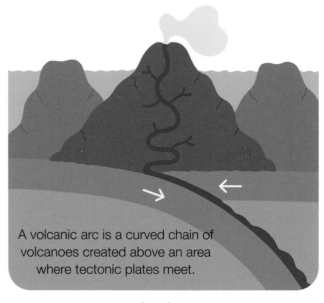

A volcanic arc is a curved chain of volcanoes created above an area where tectonic plates meet.

volcanic arc

🏠 Earthquake

Earthquakes can be caused by two plates rubbing against each other.

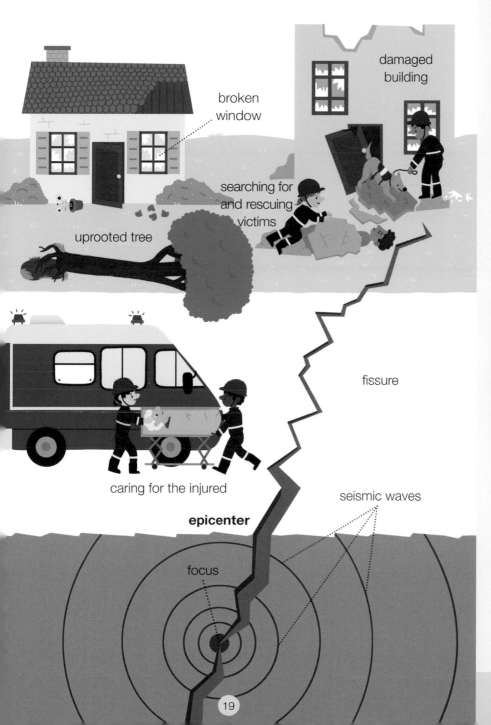

broken window

damaged building

searching for and rescuing victims

uprooted tree

caring for the injured

fissure

epicenter

seismic waves

focus

A tsunami is a series of giant waves in the ocean that are very powerful and can destroy everything when it hits land.

The waves are caused by earthquakes or volcanic eruptions on the seafloor. As the waves radiate away from the focus, they grow bigger.

Have you ever kicked so hard in a pool that water splashed out? That is similar to how a tsunami crashes onto a shore.

🐚 The Ocean

When Earth's crust stretches out, it gets thinner and forms a rift. Over time, water can fill this giant gap to create an ocean.

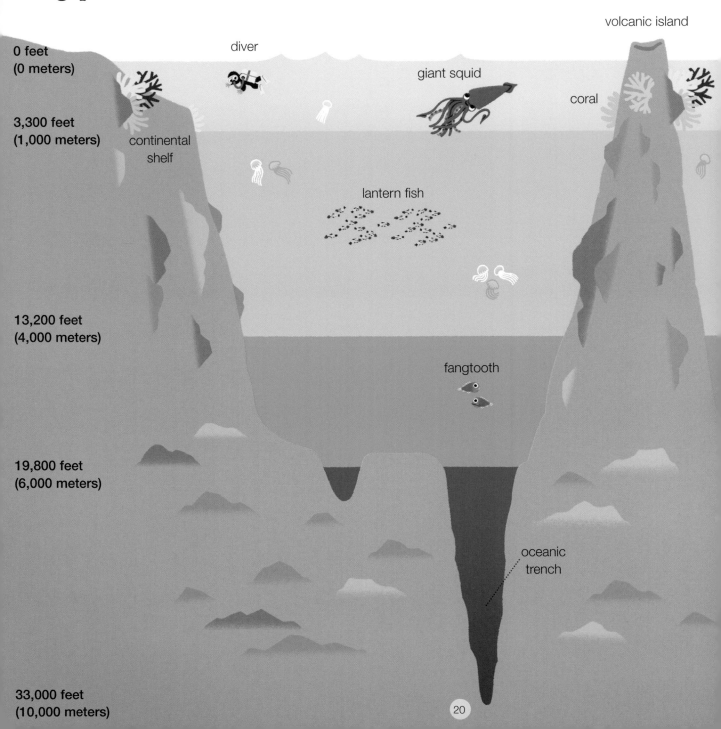

volcanic island

diver

giant squid

coral

**0 feet
(0 meters)**

**3,300 feet
(1,000 meters)**

continental shelf

lantern fish

**13,200 feet
(4,000 meters)**

fangtooth

**19,800 feet
(6,000 meters)**

oceanic trench

**33,000 feet
(10,000 meters)**

What is fresh water ?

sailboat

jellyfish

barreleye

sperm whales

seamount

anglerfish

abyssal plain

Rainwater dissolves the salt in rocks on land, which washes into the ocean and makes its water salty.

On the other hand, the water in rivers and rain contains very little salt. We call this water fresh water. The water frozen in glaciers is fresh water too.

The salt that you use on food came from the evaporation of water from various sources of salt water.

salt

Mountains

Millions of years ago, the movement of plates caused landmasses to collide, which created mountains. The shapes of mountains can change over time because of soil or weather erosion.

mountain range

glacier

stream

waterfall

lake

pasture

hill

trail

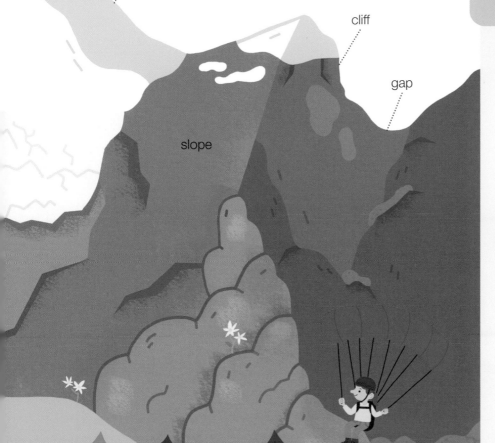

summit

ridge

cliff

gap

slope

valley

village

In the winter, snow falls on mountaintops. It piles up along the sides, or slopes, of the mountains.

When the wind blows hard or there's a big snowfall, or even when the air suddenly warms up, the snow can slide down the slopes.

In an avalanche, a huge amount of snow sweeps downhill at an incredible speed, pushing away everything in its path.

🌋 A Volcano Erupts

The movements of the plates in Earth's crust can also create volcanoes, which form when magma, or molten rock, from deep underground spews out. Magma that reaches the surface is called lava.

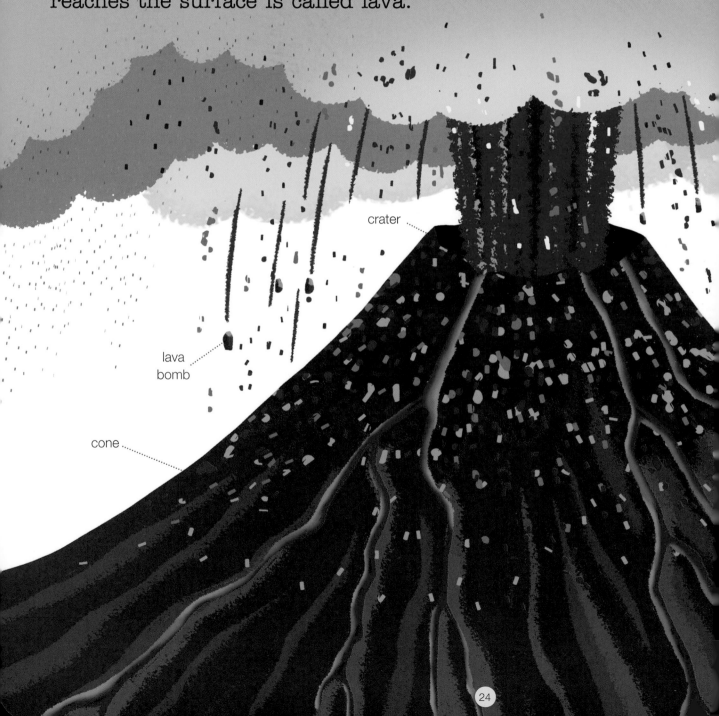

crater

lava
bomb

cone

clouds of ash

ashfall

Hot gases escape from fumaroles, openings in Earth's crust.

lava flow

Where
are volcanoes on other planets
?

When you look at images of Mars, you'll see lines and circles on the surface of the planet.

Those are volcanoes, which exist on other planets as well. They can be long dormant or still quite active.

Some of them are huge. Olympus Mons on Mars is about 370 miles (600 kilometers) wide. That's about how long Arizona is from north to south!

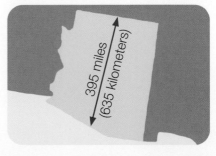

395 miles (635 kilometers)

Rocks and Minerals

Rocks make up a large part of Earth. They are nonliving pieces of materials that contain one mineral or a mixture of several minerals.

rocks

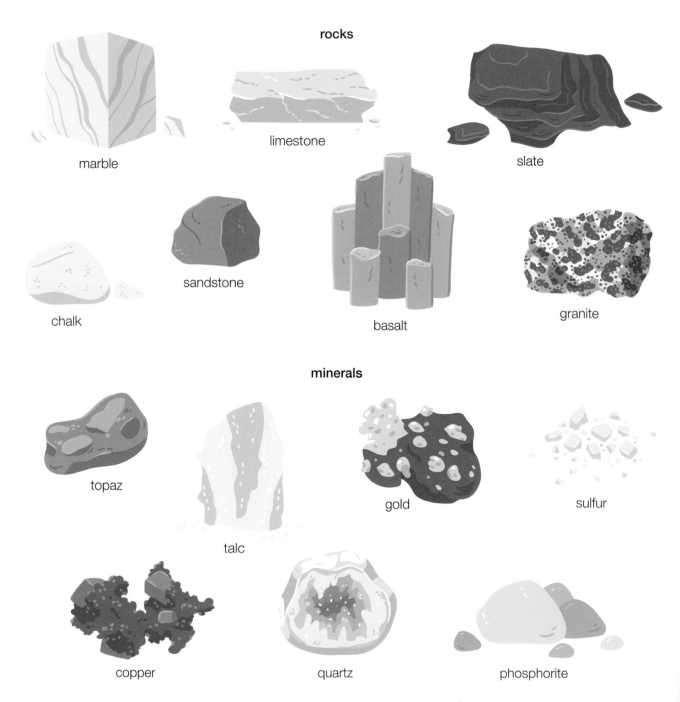

marble

limestone

slate

chalk

sandstone

basalt

granite

minerals

topaz

talc

gold

sulfur

copper

quartz

phosphorite

🐚 Fossils

Fossils are proof of the living creatures and plants that have lived on Earth. The remains can be parts of plants or animals, including bones, feathers, and even poop.

fern

ammonite

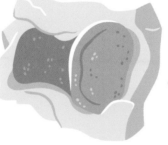

dinosaur bone

trilobite

giant dragonfly

sturgeon

hyena poop

Have you ever been to a hot desert? The Sahara is Earth's largest hot desert. Little rain falls there, and it has enormous piles of sand called dunes.

The temperature can vary from extremely hot during the day to very cold at night. The dry wind wears away the rocks, producing sand.

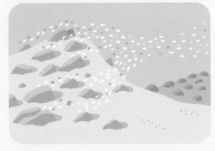

Sandy areas of deserts are called ergs, while gravelly areas are called regs.

Let's Review!

Can you name the eight planets that revolve around the Sun in our solar system? Which planet is closest to the Sun? Which is farthest away?

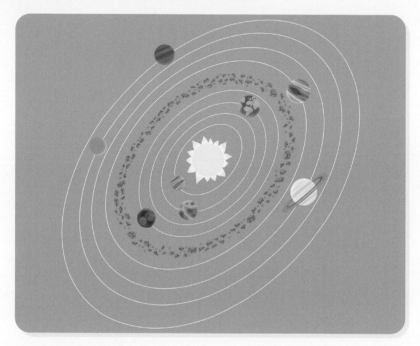

Can you tell what is happening in this scene? What caused the damage?

Which of these are minerals, and which are fossils? How are they different?

How many continents are there?
What are their names?
Which continent do you live on?

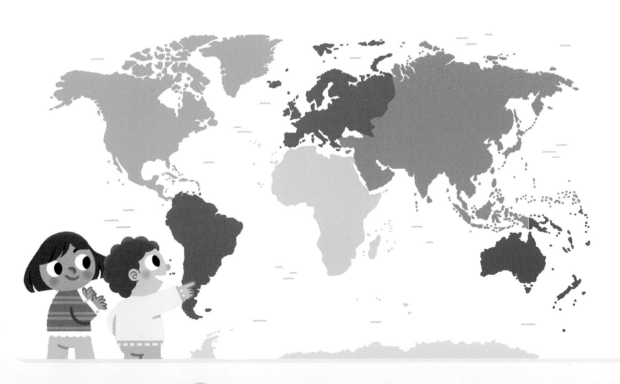

Natural Events

◐ Day and Night

During the day, the Sun lights up and warms the side of Earth facing it. At night, that same side of Earth is mostly dark.

day

magpie

napping

studying insects

cat

night

owl

sleeping

eating

dew

hedgehog

32

Sun

heat

playing

open flower
petals

bee

collecting nectar
and pollen

Moon

stars

closed flower
petals

hunting

mouse

Why
isn't it the same time everywhere
?

When you're having breakfast, it might be lunchtime for a friend who lives far away. The time where you are is different from where they are.

Earth's rotation on its own axis means that the Sun doesn't light up the whole planet at the same time.

So when it is morning in one place, it could be afternoon or night in another. Do you know what time it is in different countries around the world?

The Solar System **10**

Seasons **38**

☁ Weather

Is it going to be warm or cool today? Will you need rain boots or sandals? To find out what the weather will be, you can look up at the sky and clouds.

hot

rainy

rainbow after the rain

cold

windy

stormy

foggy

snowy

How

can people predict the weather ?

Every day, you can find out about the weather in many areas. Meteorologists study weather conditions and Earth's atmosphere to forecast the weather.

With the help of supercomputers, these scientists compile data from weather stations around the world.

The data is gathered by measuring temperature, wind speed, air pressure, and other weather conditions.

Seasons **38**
Wind **40**

Climate

Climate is the usual weather conditions in a region. Earth's climates can be hot, temperate, or cold.

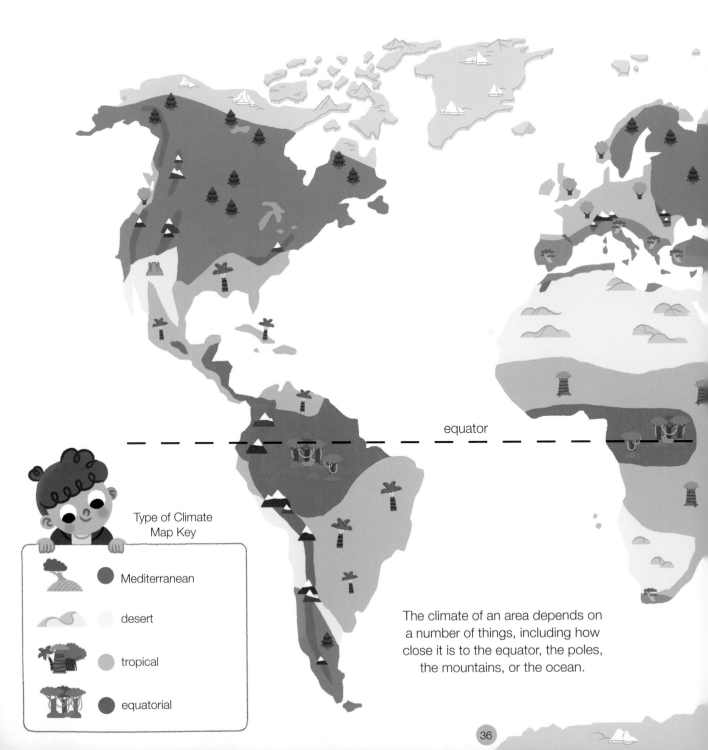

equator

Type of Climate Map Key

- Mediterranean
- desert
- tropical
- equatorial

The climate of an area depends on a number of things, including how close it is to the equator, the poles, the mountains, or the ocean.

Type of Climate Map Key

- polar
- mountain
- continental
- temperate

What is climate change?

Climate change is the rise in sea levels and in temperatures in the air and oceans, changing weather patterns, and extreme weather conditions.

Activities such as burning fossil fuels, including coal and oil, lead to more greenhouse gases in the atmosphere, causing climate change.

Everyone—governments, businesses, and people—can do their part to reduce the amount of greenhouse gases in the air. What can you do to help?

Seasons **38**
Animal Migrations **60**

🌳 Seasons

In temperate regions of the world, there are four seasons in a year. In tropical zones, there are two: a dry season and a rainy season.

Tree buds begin to open.

flowers

spring

Fruits on the tree ripen.

Sun

summer

rain

Leaves fall.

mushrooms

autumn

snow

The tree is bare.

winter

rainy season

rain

lots of food

green grass

The pond is full of water.

dry season

lack of food

dry grass

The pond is nearly empty.

What
is the summer solstice ?

In the winter, there are fewer hours of daylight. When you get up to go to school, it's still dark out. But by the end of spring, the Sun is out before you wake up!

The summer solstice is the first day of summer. That's the day with the most hours of daylight.

On two days each year, the spring and autumn equinoxes, the hours of daylight and darkness are about equal.

🪁 Wind

Wind is the movement of air. It can be gentle or harsh, hot or cold, dry or damp.

breeze: a light wind

north wind: cold and dry

sirocco: a hot, dry wind

trade winds: steady winds around the equator

🌀 Hurricane

This is a giant swirling storm with extremely strong, gusty winds. Hurricanes bring lots of rain and cause a great deal of damage.

roof shingles ripped off

damaged tree

windows boarded up

broken railing

debris

wrecked cars

cleaning up

flooding

You may have heard or read about the powerful hurricanes named Katrina, Harvey, and Ida. The World Meteorological Organization names hurricanes.

The first storm of each hurricane season, which begins on June 1, starts with the letter A. The name of the next hurricane will start with B, and so on.

Meteorologists will warn of any approaching hurricanes in your area so that everyone can make plans to keep safe.

Moving Water

Water exists on Earth in many forms and is always moving. It gushes, runs, evaporates, freezes, and melts, finding its way into tiny cracks as well as huge oceans.

Water freezes.

snow

glacier

icefall

mountain stream

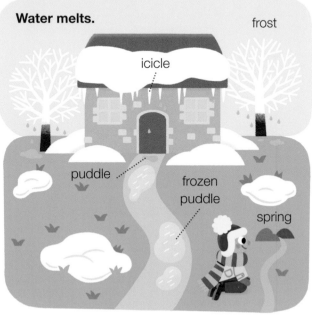

Water melts.

frost

icicle

puddle

frozen puddle

spring

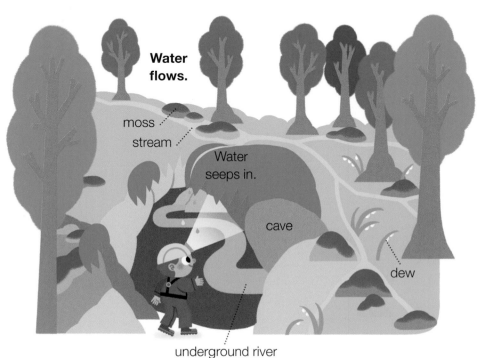

Water flows.

moss

stream

Water seeps in.

cave

dew

underground river

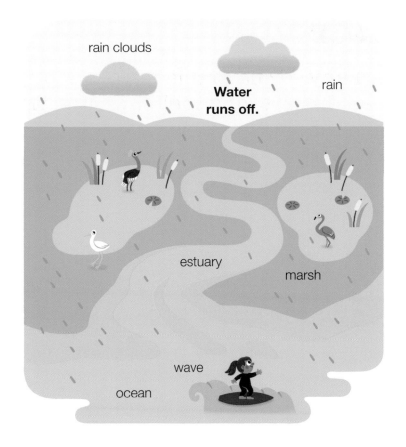

rain clouds

Water runs off.

rain

estuary

marsh

wave

ocean

Water boils and evaporates.

geyser

water vapor

hot spring

When it rains, you'll see that the rainwater is absorbed by the ground.

The water can end up in an underground lake and come out again somewhere else through a hole in the surface called a spring.

The spring can get bigger and become a stream. Water from several streams can form a river, which might lead to a bigger river that empties into the ocean.

Tides

The rotation of Earth and the Moon's gravitational pull affect the rise and fall of sea levels. This occurs because of the tide cycle.

high tide

fish

boat

buoy

wave

boat floating

playing in the water

What
are tides
?

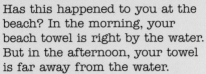

low tide

crab

rock

mussels

picking up
seashells

tide pool

catching
shrimp

boat on dry
ground

tidemark

Has this happened to you at the beach? In the morning, your beach towel is right by the water. But in the afternoon, your towel is far away from the water.

The water level changes about twice a day. When the Moon is close to Earth, its tidal force pulls water toward it, and sea levels rise. This is high tide.

When the Moon is farther away from Earth, sea levels go down. This is low tide.

Amazing Sky Displays

Sometimes spectacular events appear in the sky. They are called natural phenomena.

rainbow

lightning

total solar eclipse

total lunar eclipse

shooting star

light pillars

polar lights

mammatus clouds

nacreous or mother-of-pearl clouds

lenticular clouds

hole punch cloud

Kelvin-Helmholtz wave cloud

What
is a shooting star ?

On a clear night, you might see a bright streak in the sky. It's a shooting star! What flies across is not a star, but small rocks called meteoroids.

The ones that enter our atmosphere and burn up, creating a trail of bright light, are called meteors.

When many meteors shoot through the sky in a group, it's called a meteor shower. Have you ever seen one?

The Solar System **10**
Weather **34**

Let's Review!

What time of day do these two pictures show? How do you know?

Can you put the four seasons in order, starting with spring?

Match each cloud with its shadow. Do you know the names of the clouds?

What types of winds are shown in these pictures?
How are they different?

Life on
Our Planet

⇄ Underground

On or in the ground, lots of critters are busy making humus, the nutrient-rich dirt that helps plants grow.

mole

fallen leaves

fox poop

worm cast

wood louse

springtails

seed

earthworm

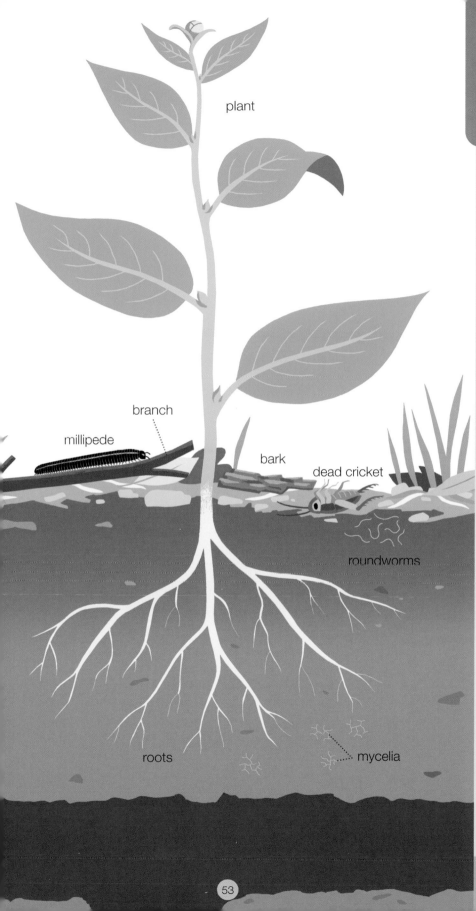

plant

branch

millipede

bark

dead cricket

roundworms

roots

mycelia

How
do earthworms help the soil

?

Have you ever found an earthworm while digging in the ground? These creatures are also called night crawlers.

Earthworms feed on the remains of plants—roots and leaves— as well as animal poop. After digesting this food, they create their own poop called worm casts.

The worm casts make nutrients easy for plants to absorb, and keep the soil moist. When worms burrow, they also help air and water move better in the soil.

Seasons **38**

Farming Close to Home **82**

🌲 In the Forest

A forest is an area of land where there is a large population of trees. There are different types of forests, each with its own native plants and animals.

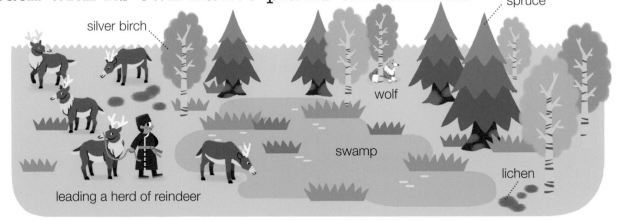

silver birch

spruce

wolf

swamp

lichen

leading a herd of reindeer

boreal forest

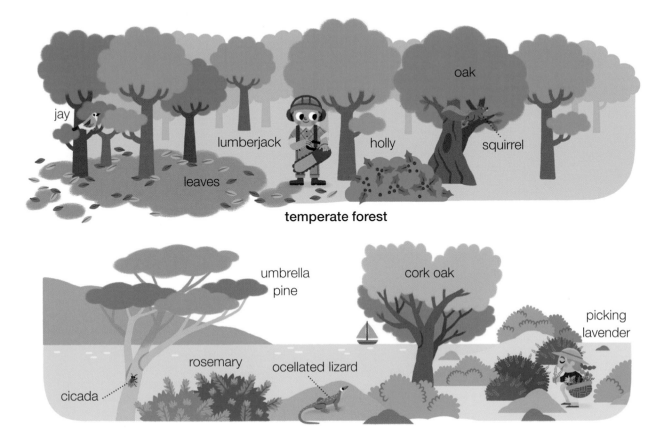

jay

oak

lumberjack

holly

squirrel

leaves

temperate forest

umbrella pine

cork oak

picking lavender

rosemary

ocellated lizard

cicada

Mediterranean forest

the canopy

toucan

rain

liana vine

palm tree

paddling a canoe

jaguar

tropical rain forest

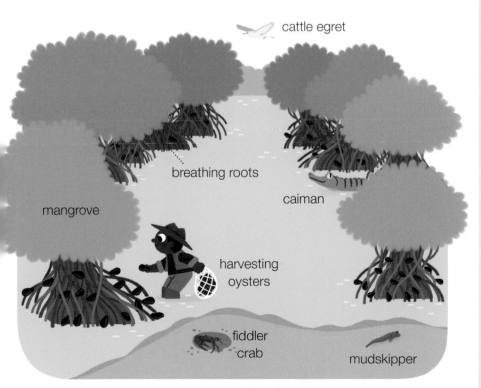

cattle egret

breathing roots

caiman

mangrove

harvesting oysters

fiddler crab

mudskipper

mangrove forest

How
do forests grow ?

The seeds of trees and plants are carried by wind or animals to other areas. They sprout and grow into new trees or plants.

In some forests, this happens naturally. But people also create forests so they can use the wood from the trees.

Wood is used for many things, including the frames and walls of houses. It is a sturdy material that provides protection.

Climate **36**
Planting Trees **80**

In the Desert

Deserts are regions where there is little rainfall and it is very hot or very cold. Some plant and animal species—including humans—have adapted to live here.

hot desert

off-road vehicle

dune

trail

oasis

fennec fox

leading a camel caravan

camels

desert horned viper

rocks

rock carving

jerboa

polar desert

snowmobile

seals

polar bear

ice sheet

walrus

scientific
research boat

iceberg

shrimp

sperm whale

What
is an iceberg
?

When it's hot, you might put an ice cube in your juice to make it cold. An iceberg is like a giant ice cube!

An iceberg is a large piece of ice that breaks off from a glacier or an ice shelf. This process is called calving. The iceberg floats in open water and may melt over time.

The idiom "It's just the tip of the iceberg" is true! Only a very small part appears above the water; most of it is under the surface.

In the Air

The sky is the great space above the surface of the earth. It is where you'll find clouds, birds, and people flying in aircraft!

hot-air balloon

stork

kestrel

butterfly

housefly

ladybug

dragonfly

sparrow

airliner

cloud

chickadee

mosquitoes

bee

How
do clouds get their shapes

?

Clouds are made up of tiny water droplets. Sometimes they look like familiar objects. Their shapes depend on the air temperature and the wind.

Air is warmer lower in the sky. The water droplets in the clouds are "wetter," so clouds look fluffy. When there's too much water in the clouds, it's released as rain.

High up in the sky, where the air is cold, the water droplets in clouds freeze, and the clouds look more like wispy feathers.

Amazing Sky Displays **46**
Animal Migrations **60**

🐧 Animal Migrations

Many species of animals take a long-distance journey at least once in their lives. This seasonal movement, alone or in a group, is called migration.

Canada geese

eating a lot of food before the long journey

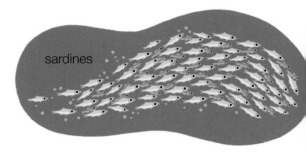
sardines

gathering together

leaving

zebras

protecting each other from predators

common cranes

flying in a V shape

wildebeest

grazing on fresh grass

sea turtle

laying eggs

arriving

swallows

flying away

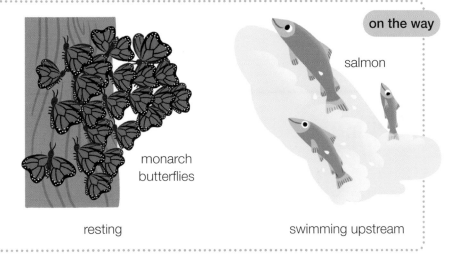

on the way

monarch butterflies

resting

salmon

swimming upstream

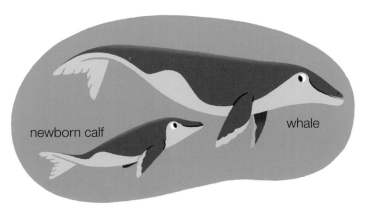

newborn calf

whale

giving birth

Have you ever seen starlings on telephone wires in the fall? They're gathering before migrating south for the winter.

Birds are able to navigate using Earth's magnetic field to sense direction. Other animals can use the Sun, stars, and smells to help them.

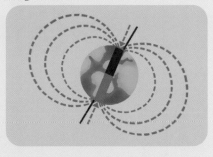

Some elephants migrate when seasons change, traveling to find fresh food. The older elephants create pathways for the younger ones to follow.

Children of the World

There are more than 7 billion people on Earth today, and more than 2 billion of them are children. They all eat, sleep, and play—although perhaps in a different way than you do.

eating

with knives, forks, and spoons   with chopsticks   with hands

sleeping

bed

futon

dressing

sari   boubou

playing

piñata

hopscotch

mancala

going to school

on foot

on a bus

in a car

by bicycle

learning

with a teacher

with a family member

with a book

on a computer

What
do children learn at school ?

At school, you make friends and learn to play with them. You also learn lots of things with your teacher.

Your teacher might teach you about Earth and about science and nature.

You are taught to read and write, and maybe even study a different language.

Life on Earth **8**
Protecting Our Planet **88**

❄ Playing Outdoors

For many children, the outdoors is an exciting place to play and explore, whether it's a backyard, a park, or the beach.

playing with snow

tree house

climbing a tree

playing in mud

making
a sandcastle

finding
seashells

skipping stones

looking for
smooth rocks

What
is land art

?

In the woods, you may have had fun picking up and arranging leaves, twigs, moss, and bark on the ground.

This activity is called land art. It is the creation of beautiful shapes with what you find in nature.

To always remember what you've made, you can ask a grown-up to help you take a picture—before the wind blows it away!

🚴 Discovering Our Planet

Earth is full of amazing places to explore, and there are many activities that allow us to do this on land, in the water, and even in the air.

mountaineering

spelunking

paragliding

hiking

cycling

orienteering

surfing

land sailing

snorkeling

canoeing

rafting

canyoneering

You may have read exciting stories about pirates who bury treasure on desert islands.

Desert islands are islands that people don't inhabit permanently. There are many such islands scattered around the world, mostly in remote locations.

Because these islands can be hard for people to get to, they become safe places for many animals and plants.

Let's Review!

Can you identify the following things in this picture: springtails, leaves, earthworms, worm cast? What animal is coming out of its hole?

What creatures and object are shown below on the left? Where would you place them in the picture?

These pictures show animals on a journey called a migration. Can you name the animals?

What types of activities are shown here?
Where can they be done?

Taking Care
of Earth

🔍 Studying Our Planet

Scientists in many fields study Earth closely to know it well. By understanding our planet, people can find ways to take care of it.

geologist: studies Earth and its structure and processes

oceanographer: studies the ocean

volcanologist: studies volcanoes and volcanic activity

botanist: studies plants

zoologist: studies animals

climatologist: studies climates

Guarding Our Planet

Many people work to make sure Earth flourishes and continues to be a healthy home for all living creatures.

nature educator: teaches others about plants and animals

community activist: defends nature

judge: uses the law to protect nature

reporter and documentary maker: raise awareness through the media

park ranger: makes sure people follow the rules

Many neighborhoods encourage recycling by setting up bins for certain materials, such as glass bottles, plastic containers, paper, and metal cans.

Governments can create protected natural spaces and support businesses that engage in sustainable farming, which reduces environmental damage.

Materials that cause pollution can be banned. These may include plastic straws, which often end up in oceans and waterways.

Rocks and Minerals **26**
Eco-friendly Areas **86**

☣ Destruction of Nature

People sometimes engage in practices that are harmful to the environment.

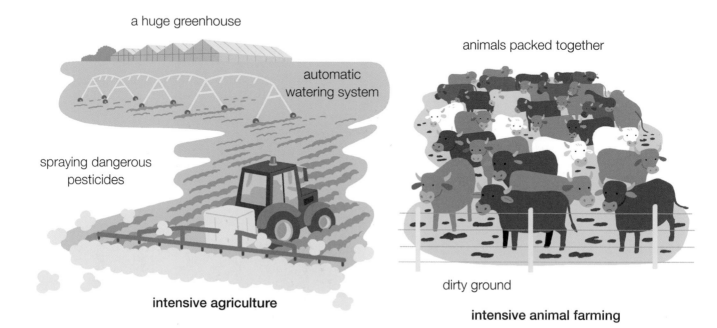

a huge greenhouse

automatic watering system

spraying dangerous pesticides

intensive agriculture

animals packed together

dirty ground

intensive animal farming

running away

burning the forest

cutting down trees

building a road through the forest

deforestation

coal mining

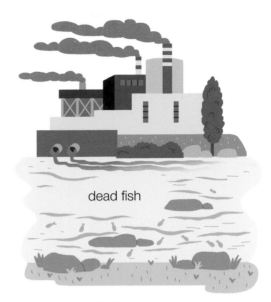

polluted rivers

dead fish

oil wells

oil spill

bird covered in oil

large fishing boat

huge net

overfishing

Planting Trees **80**
Pollution in the City **84**

Endangered Animals

Many species of animals are the victims of overfishing, hunting, and pollution. These animals seek shelter in other areas, but their lands continue to disappear.

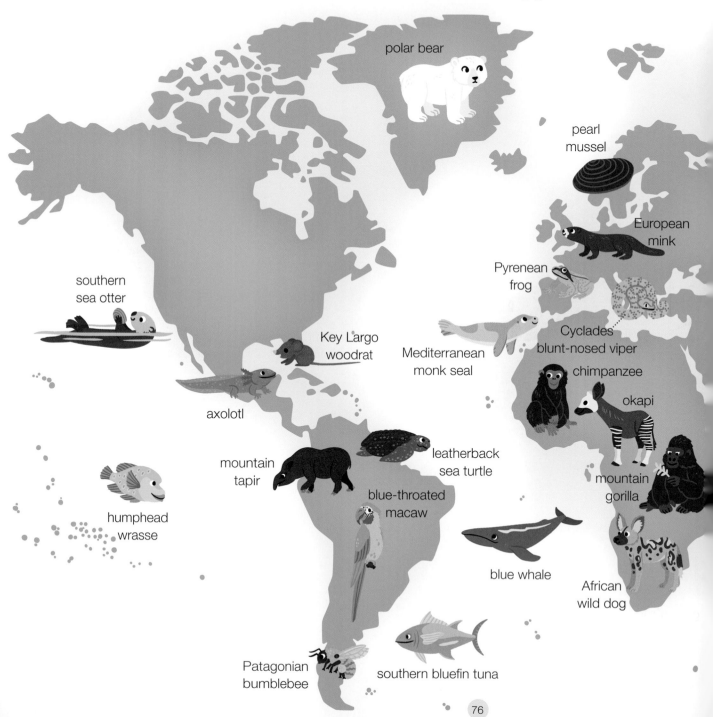

polar bear

pearl mussel

European mink

Pyrenean frog

Cyclades blunt-nosed viper

chimpanzee

okapi

southern sea otter

Key Largo woodrat

Mediterranean monk seal

mountain gorilla

axolotl

leatherback sea turtle

mountain tapir

blue-throated macaw

humphead wrasse

blue whale

African wild dog

Patagonian bumblebee

southern bluefin tuna

Why

do people kill animals

?

In many countries, hunting is a sport that takes place in hunting preserves. There, hunters chase wild animals, including elk, bighorn sheep, and ducks.

People who hunt wild animals illegally are called poachers. They kill creatures, such as the rhinoceros, to make money from selling their body parts.

Cows, chickens, and other animals are raised on farms to be eaten. Their meat is usually sold in grocery stores.

saiga

giant panda

gharial

pangolin

great hammerhead shark

tiger

orangutan

rhinoceros

Taom striped gecko

swift parrot

Maui dolphin

golden mantella

kiwi

Destruction of Nature **74**

Conservation Areas **78**

Conservation Areas

There are protected areas where it is against the law to hunt wild animals or destroy vegetation. Injured animals may be treated at special care centers.

nature reserve

marine protected area

care center: treating injured animals

sanctuary: raising orphaned baby animals

wildlife garden

What
is a wildlife crossing ?

To cross the street safely, you use a crosswalk. In many areas around the world, crosswalks for wild animals have been constructed.

Wildlife crossings are safe paths between spaces that certain species of animals use regularly. These areas might be separated by a highway or a railroad track.

The special passageways are used by animals such as bears, elephants, turtles, toads, and even crabs.

🌱 Planting Trees

Trees are an essential part of nature. Different types of trees can be raised on a farm and then replanted in many places so they can continue to provide food, clean the air, prevent soil erosion, and offer shelter to animals.

preparing the soil

placing trees in the planting holes

How

do trees "breathe" ?

protecting and watering the trees

allowing trees to grow

Trees are living things. They "breathe," or respire through tiny pores on their leaves called stomata.

Leaves absorb carbon dioxide—the gas we breathe out—and other gases that pollute the air, and change them into oxygen.

Have you noticed that the air smells and feels fresh when you're walking around trees? It even feels cooler.

Farming Close to Home

If you have a backyard or a small plot in a community garden, you can grow fruits and vegetables, without using harmful chemicals, fertilizers, or pesticides.

small plot of land

wildflower garden

broadfork

turning over the soil

growing and storing plants in a greenhouse

hedge: protects plants from wind

lentils: create nitrogen-rich soil

carrots

mulch: keeps moisture in the soil

tomatoes

compost bin: breaks down fruit and vegetable scraps into compost

ladybugs: eat pests such as aphids

compost: a natural fertilizer

flower bed

What
is organic fruit

?

Fruits, vegetables, and grains can be grown organically. Animals, such as chickens and cows, can also be raised so the eggs and milk they produce are organic.

Organic foods at the store will have a special sign to let you know they were either grown or raised organically.

Organic fruits are grown without artificial chemicals, pesticides, and other harmful substances. There are specific rules for fruit tree orchards.

Seasons 38
Underground 52

🗑 Pollution in the City

Filled with people, vehicles, noise, and constant activity, cities have a lot of pollution in the air, the ground, and the waters.

wholesale center

truck

highway interchange

SUPERMARKET

ENTRANCE

164 JFH

341 ABC

196 CLL

used packaging

70% off

digital billboard

plastic bag

commercial district

exhaust fumes

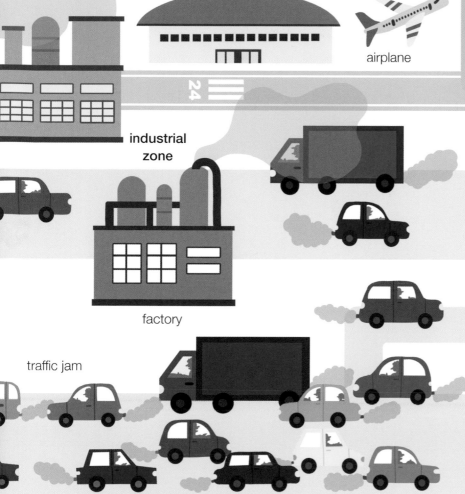

airport

airplane

industrial zone

factory

traffic jam

highway

neon sign

PIZZA

bad smells

garbage

The Sun provides natural light during the day. At night, we depend on artificial light. But when you go to bed, you turn out the lights in your room.

The darkness helps you fall asleep. Too much artificial light has a negative impact on the health of humans and animals.

To lessen light pollution, more cities are making changes by using motion-sensitive lighting and light bulbs with lower wattage.

Eco-friendly Areas

In a growing number of cities, there are neighborhoods that plan ways to protect the environment.

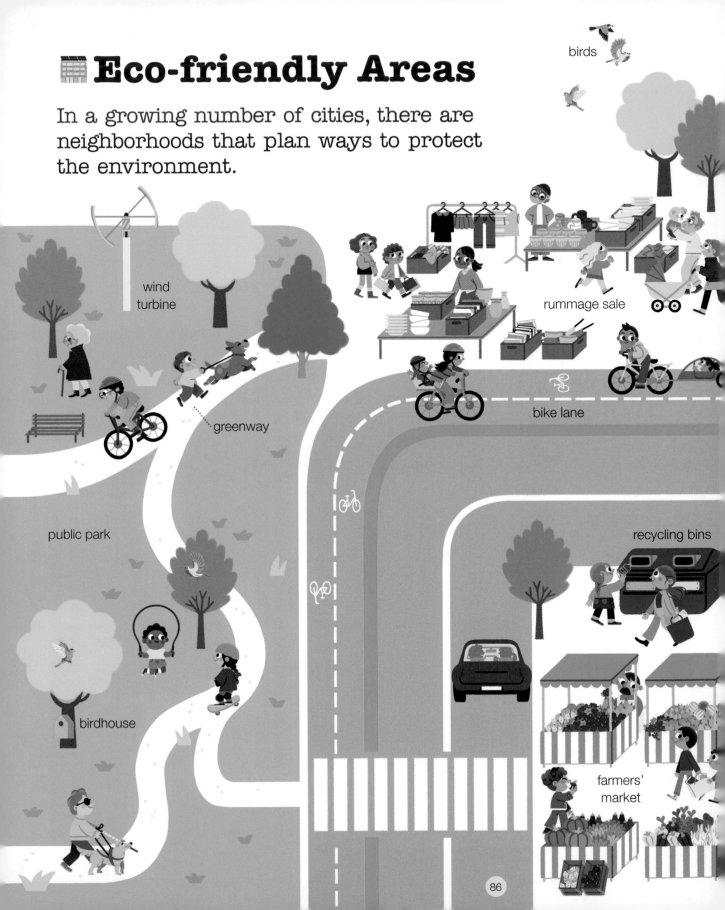

birds

wind turbine

rummage sale

bike lane

greenway

public park

recycling bins

birdhouse

farmers' market

solar panel

green roof

collecting rainwater

sidewalk

electric bus

compost bin

community garden

What
is renewable energy ?

You use energy every day to turn on the lights, watch TV, or run hot water.

Renewable energy is energy that comes from natural sources and will not run out. These include wind, water, and solar energy, which is energy from the Sun.

Petroleum, natural gas, and coal are forms of nonrenewable energy. There is a limited supply on Earth, and once it is used up, there isn't any more.

Studying Our Planet 72
Protecting Our Planet 88

 Protecting Our Planet

Children can help protect Earth. Every day, whether at home, school, or anywhere else you go, you can take steps to care for our planet.

take a quick shower

grow a scented herb garden

turn off the tap

sorting recyclables

32

cook with local produce

prepare your own snacks

travel by walking or biking

turn off
the lights

borrow toys from
a toy library

500 pieces

turn off the TV

use both sides
of the paper

How
can you avoid wasting electricity ?

You've often heard grown-ups say not to waste water or electricity. To waste something is to take or use something when you don't need it.

Leaving lights on in an empty room wastes electricity.

Pollution is reduced when electricity, water, or food is not wasted. So take a second to turn off the light!

Let's Review!

Do you know where each of these endangered animals originally came from?

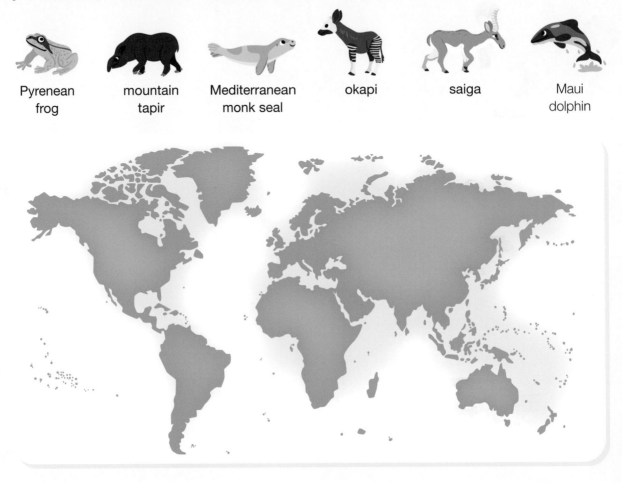

Pyrenean frog

mountain tapir

Mediterranean monk seal

okapi

saiga

Maui dolphin

How are these activities helping to protect Earth?

How do each of these people help take care of Earth?

nature educator

park ranger

geologist

zoologist

judge

What are these children doing to protect the planet?

Index

S

Sahara 27
saiga 77
salmon 61
salt water 21
sanctuary 79
sand 27
sandstone 26
sardine 60
sari 62
Saturn 10
scientific research boat 57
Scotia Plate 16
sea 13
sea turtle 60
seal 57
seamount 21
seashell 45, 65
seed 52-55
seismic wave 19
shrimp 45, 57
sidewalk 87
silver birch 54
sirocco 40
slate 26
slope 23
snorkeling 66
snow 35, 38, 42, 64
snowmobile 57
solar panel 87
solar system 10
South America 14
South American Plate 16
southern bluefin tuna 76
Southern Ocean 14
southern sea otter 76
sparrow 58
spelunking 66
sperm whale 21, 57
sponge 12
spring (season) 38
spring (water source) 42, 43
springtail 52
spruce 54
squirrel 54
star 10, 33, 46, 47, 61
starling 61
stomata 81
stork 58
stream 22, 42, 43
sturgeon 27
sulfur 26
summer 38, 39

summit 23
Sun 8, 10, 11, 32–33, 38, 61, 85, 87
surfing 66
swallow 61
swamp 54
swift parrot 77

T

talc 26
Taom striped gecko 77
tectonic plate 16, 18, 19, 22, 24
temperate forest 54
tide 44–45
tide pool 45
tidemark 45
tiger 77
tomato 83
topaz 26
toucan 55
trade wind 40
traffic jam 85
trilobite 27
tropical rain forest 55
truck 84
tsunami 19

U

umbrella pine 54
Uranus 10

V

valley 23
Venus 10
village 23
volcanic arc 18
volcanic island 20
volcano 18, 19, 24–25, 72
volcanologist 72

W

walrus 57
water vapor 43
waterfall 22
wave 43, 44
weather 34–35
whale 21, 57, 61
wholesale center 84
wildebeest 60
wildflower garden 82
wildlife crossing 79
wildlife garden 79
wind 40
wind turbine 86
winter 38, 39, 61
wolf 54
wood louse 52
worm cast 52, 53

Z

zebra 60
zoologist 72